# *Tin Ears*

*By Gregory Powell*

**BW** *Broad Wing Press ©2020*

Capitol Heights, Maryland

Tin Ears

Copyright © 2020 Broad Wing Press

All rights reserved.

Printed in the United States

ISBN-13: 978-1-938373-35-0
LCCN: 2020931912

All rights reserved. No part of this book may be reproduced in any form, except for the inclusion of brief quotations in a review, without permission in writing from the author or publisher.

# Contents

| | |
|---|---|
| Dedication | i |
| Acknowledgements | ii |
| The 1960s | 1 |
| Prophet of Mercy Street | 2 |
| Second Fiddle | 4 |
| Creation | 6 |
| Elementary Education | 9 |
| Ted the Rooster | 11 |
| If this Rooster Owned a mirror | 12 |
| Red Bike | 13 |
| Faking It | 15 |
| A Smart Bird | 17 |
| Sweet to the Bone: A Biography | 19 |
| First Day | 24 |
| Butter Knife | 25 |
| Mr. Tin Ears | 26 |
| Lead Belly | 28 |
| Hope | 30 |
| Camel Knees | 31 |
| Prayer Chain | 32 |
| Lunch | 33 |
| Blue Plate | 36 |
| Canary | 37 |

| | |
|---|---|
| Leather Seats | 38 |
| Hunger Bone | 40 |
| The Size of a Cowpea | 43 |
| Blame it on the Blues | 45 |
| Knee Babies | 45 |
| Brothers in bone | 47 |
| Upon Seeing My First Kiss | 48 |
| Falcon | 49 |
| Haiku | 51 |
| Brogans | 52 |
| Underwriter (stocks, bonds, blues, etc., etc) | 54 |
| Fastback | 56 |
| Final Blue Note | 58 |
| Prophecy | 60 |
| The Last Supper | 62 |
| Sweet Honey in the Rock | 65 |
| Grace | 67 |
| Epilogue: Morning Psalm | 69 |
| About the Author | 71 |

## *Dedication*

This collection of poems is dedicated to my parents, Florence Williams Powell and Franklin Powell Sr. (a/k/a Red), both of whom taught me how to sing these songs of survival in this *strange land,* even with tin ears.

> "…But since I knew you trusted and believed,
> I could not disappoint you and so prevailed."

From Paul Laurence Dunbar, "Encouraged," in *Lyrics of Sunshine and Shadow.* (New York: Dodd, Mead & Company, 1905)

## *Acknowledgements*

Special thanks to Dr. Estrelda Alexander, President of William Seymour College, Artist Della Wells who created the cover art; Artist Quez Shipman of Birmingham who photographed the cover art, and Varnessa Barnes who read an early draft of this manuscript and offered great advice. Thanks to my poetry editor, Evette Keene. Thanks to Robin Behn and the Creative Writing Department at the University of Alabama-Tuscaloosa. Blessings to you and your families…continue to walk in the light.

## *The 1960s*
*For Debra*

Colored girls sky-gaze for

Cardinals slicing, gliding

Through Memphis skies,

Thickening with black smoke

Belched from those smokestacks


Of greasy factories downtown. When

they spot a brave red bird crest then roll

Girls in the neighborhood blow kisses

("Blow a kiss to a red bird and

Get a brand new red dress!").


In Spring, the Memphis sky

Is a sheet of red velvet, cantilevered

On sweet colored kisses & faith,

Stretching from our front porches

To the front steps of heaven.

## *Prophet of Mercy Street*

If she doesn't hum
The simple biscuits

In her stove will not
Rise (nor will the sun).

Her lips are chapped.
She closes her eyes

& her mind staggers
Under the weight of

Its own limitations; the Spirit
Then loosens her brass tongue;

It almost unhinges
In expectation;

Her mind, earlier a blank canvas, reels & pitches
As He writes His plan on her compliant tongue;

She sees her sister - peeling the moon

As if it's a banana, revealing a baby boy;

Though he refuses her sister's sweet milk

He licks & sucks ancient texts soaked in balm.

She reaches for her next breath

But draws back an empty hand:

Her biscuits will be light today

But it will be her last batch.

## *Second Fiddle*

Heavy with expectation,

She stands on her front porch.

As she yawns, Summer changes

To Fall; each pearl-drop of sweat

Weighs a pound. Weighs a ton.

It seems she's been pregnant

For two straight years. Her ankles,

Two swelling ham hocks,

Spill-over patent leather oxfords.

It seems she's been tumbling big

For four straight years.


She takes a seat

In a cane-bottomed chair

That's held each

Pregnant woman in her family,

Some twice her size.

But the chair never complains,

A sweet chariot,

Eternally accommodating.

She begins tapping her feet,

Passing good times & rhythm

To her unborn son through her feet.


Then, a mocking bird perches in a cherry tree,

Listening. A repetitious bird

Drawn to the rhythm section

Of the woman's feet.

She continues tapping

To two different rhythms.

As if two records spin

On two separate turntables in her brain;

A quarter on each hand

Steadies needles in her vinyl groove

& signals her son to crown.

## *Creation*

I peek inside our hen house.

I sneak inside. Nose around.

No hens stirring. No rooster watching.

It's hot – firecracker hot.

Sweat streams down my face,

A personal river running down my back

Separating sharp shoulder blades

Into two tender Tennessee bluffs.

Salting backbone. Seasoning my ribs.

Splitting my cheeks in half-moons.

I stand on the tips of my toes &

Peek inside the constellation

Of golden straw of Rose's nest.

My curious nose levels with sweated straw

& a hen's damp feathers.

A few days earlier, my mom had set Rose

On a clutch of seven white eggs.

Rose became the Queen of Sheba

In this hot hen-house blues.

Reigning over a living elegy of

Shell, membrane, yellow yolk & time.

Then, Mom shaded white eggs

with my fat first-grade pencil,

Which I'd used to write the elementary letters

Of my name. Rose's eggs slowly

Turned into lead in her hands.

Days later, baby chicks dart

Around Rose's perfect nest.

I lift one.

Rub it across my nose/cheeks.

I had worried about the chicks.

Mom warned that I was too young to worry.

Little boys who worry awake with old men's eyes

In their young heads.

I like my eyes -

Better than I'd like another's eyes in my head.

With another's eyes, I'd have to relearn

My letters/colors (not to mention the moon)

Because I'd be seeing them

For the first time with another's eyes.

So, I stop worrying & start

Wondering more than I'd worried:

Wonder if mom had used the eraser-end

Of my pencil could she have erased

All traces of the seven eggs from the nest,

Leaving straw & time for Rose to incubate?

Wonder if I had eaten a shaded egg

Would I have turned into lead?

## *Elementary Education*

In the second grade
    I am more vinegar
Than boy. If a cardinal had lighted
    On a fence I lifted
A feather without the bird
    Blinking. When I sweated
It was not because I was tired
    But because I'd given my sweat
Permission to sweat.
    There was nothing else to do.
Nowhere to go.
    No new woods to roam.
A lumpy oatmeal
    Kind of day, 24 greyed hours.


One morning, I'd chased hens
    Around the front & back yards.
Mom warned me
    That chased hens
Would become confused,

    Laying eggs in the yard/

In a tree/in a shoe. Everywhere.

    Anywhere but in their cribs.

And our dogs would eat

    These eggs & egg-eating dogs would

Become chicken-eating dogs.

    And if that happened I had hell to pay.

And since she was no bank,

    She wouldn't accept no check from me.

Only my butt would settle the bill.

*Ted the Rooster*

We are life-long enemies every day. I scout our farm armed with a slingshot & a pocketful of ball bearings. While Ted scratches out a living with spurs which could slice shinbone/ fieldstone/ breastbone & tombstone. He has one eye trained on me & his other pinned on the prizes & pretties he spurs from our dirt-packed concrete yard. Ted's eyes are two black ball bearings.

Now, he looks at me as if I am one of those lazy worms he'd just spurred from the ground. If he had only been born with one eye, or just one lazy eye. While Ted can see from Memphis to heaven, I need eyeglasses to see a glass of water set before me. Ted is cucumber cool, because he never gives himself permission to sweat. If he corners me, my only path of escape will be flight. I'm sweating ball bearings.

## *If this Rooster Owned a Mirror*

Ted only preens his golden feathers if a hen is looking his way, or to hail the rain. His perfect beak prinks & primps each silk feather, forks through every hollow quill. Otherwise, his golden crest would be caked with every tick & bug in our yard. Ted's tail feathers are dripping-blood red; he is a suitor in red gators. He loves to turn his tail feathers & backside to me, most of the time. He thinks too much of himself, all of the time. Not that I'm judging this golden bird with the silk feathers, who thrives in a fool's paradise of seed & shade. Our pastor preaches that we shouldn't judge a living soul in the living world & I agree. If Ted owned a mirror, we'd never have any eggs or chicks because he'd stare at himself thirty hours a day.

*Red Bike*
*For Jewel*


From behind her desk,

My teacher announces

That we will all die

On some undetermined date

During some workweek

In some long, lonely hour

When everyone in the world

Is busy running errands.

She sucks her teeth.

Makes a clucking sound like

Our hen Rose, who clucks

To summon her clutch home

& to summon summer.

For that reason,

My teacher clucks,

We must learn our letters.


As if handing death a letter

Would fill his stomach

& buy us more time.

Filling his stomach with lowercase

Letters as Lead Belly's

Belly had been filled with lead.

She instructs us to recite

The alphabet backwards,

Beginning with Z.

Our voices rise, level off

To one screeching soprano.

She is our human metronome

Marking our time by tapping

Her yellow yardstick on the chalk board.

A redhead boy who sits in front of me

Breaks rank, tools in his nose

With his finger. I don't know

Who death is. Does he suck his teeth?

Does he even have teeth?

Maybe he gums his food like my

Sister Jewel gums yams

& corn bread soaked in pot liquor.

I may not know death's face

Or if he has a face, but if he clucks

Like Rose & my teacher

I'll hear him, and he'll never

Ever catch me & he'll never

Catch Jewel because we'll take wing

On my new red bike.

## *Faking It*

Ted crows all night long, all day long, as if Ella Fitzgerald will note the silver trumpet in his throat and register for a few of his bird-brained lessons. If this golden bird invests in a wrist watch, he would not confuse his nights and days, like my baby sister, who thinks time should bend for her because her blue bottle is empty. I know Ted is faking it. He doesn't have dropsy & he is not suffering from Alzheimer's. He knows day is day and night is night. That's his nine-to-five.

Last night, Ted had crowed every time my dad would spend Howlin' Wolf's 45 on our record player. Wolf howls & bays at a Memphis moon like his hindquarters are being crushed in the steel teeth of a bear trap. Then, Ted uncorks the silver trumpet in his throat and crows like a fool who suddenly remembers he can't swim, "after" having jumped into the middle of the muddy Mississippi River. Every time Wolf growls loud enough to shake Ted's henhouse, Ted crows. Crows as if every hen had packed her belongings & caught the last train to Chicago. All record long. All song long: from the time dad drops a quarter on the hand of the record player (so Wolf won't skip a beat) until Wolf's final growl on the world's turn table.

I'm not surprised. I'm not impressed. Ted crows when it rains too little; crows when it rains too long; crows when his coop fills with loneliness & blues; crows when the sun bakes the front yard too hard for him to spur out a square meal of worms;

crows when ice cubes circle in his silver drinking bucket & crows when his drinking water is too hot. All night long. He crows all day long. On Sunday, my pastor had preached that when Judas betrayed Jesus with a salty kiss *that that* rooster in the Bible had only crowed once & the sun rose. So I know Ted is faking it, because it only takes one crow to raise the sun.

## A Smart Bird

Ted's comb is redder than the summer

Sun which he crows up in the morning

& crows to bed in the evening

(Who pays Ted's overtime?).

Redder than the comb

That keeps my teacher's bun

Attached & anchored to her

Shoulders. Every day she wears

A different colored comb.

Without the plastic comb her head

Could fly off her narrow shoulders.

Fly off beyond heaven to Chicago

Where Big-named Black people live.

Fly off beyond where superman can fly.

Ted could teach my teacher

How to save some money

& keep her head on her shoulders at the same time:

Wear the same red comb every day.

Below Ted's golden feathers,

Circling Ted's thick neck,

Is a bracelet of red feathers,

Which melt into more gold feathers

Streaming to Ted's dry cracked feet.

His red bracelet of feathers

Reminds me of my sister's baby bib.

Which fits under her plump chin.

Protecting her clothes from

Milk stains & pot liquor spots.

Why does a rooster need a bib?

Maybe Ted wears his bib

So his red bracelet does not bleed

Onto his golden feathers?

What a smart bird.

## *Sweet to the Bone: A Biography*

Ted's cracked feet are crusted

With dirt & caked with the remains

Of the yards he patrols

In double & triple shifts.

Hens & chicks in tow.

The sun bakes the pressed dirt

In our backyard; the dirt flakes into a

Million pieces of a puzzle.

Only the rain can unscramble

These pieces (when it has some spare time

On its hand) with a downpour,

Leveling the playing field between

Ted & the simple worms he spurs.


Ted was one of seven white eggs,

Nestled in the straw world of Rose's nest.

I had watched my mom color each egg

With my yellow, first-grade pencil.

Until the eggs became a clutch of lead

& desperateness.

I'd known Ted before he was Ted,
Before he'd hatched.
When he was an egg-head
Nosing within a fluid sack for a liquid latch.
To breathe the air of his choice.
Even then, treading in his own life sack,
Ted was a clock-watcher,
Eager for his sun to rise.

One day stretches into many yolk-filled days.
Ted is the first of Rose's lead clutch to peck
Free of her embryonic embrace.
Immediately, he begins to preen his few faint feathers,
As if he is the Master of Ceremonies
Within the coliseum of Rose's nest.
I name him Ted because his head crested
Ahead of the other six eggs.
He struts around the nest as *the* Emcee,
Beyond feather-brained expectations.
Ted is born to walk the walk of the King Cock.
He is willing to pay the cost to be the Boss
Of the primrose henhouse.

Weeks pass and Ted's feathers
Turn golden in the sun. A red bracelet
Of feathers around his neck is a show-stopper.
Ted learns to flash razor-sharp spurs for the hens
Who have the commonsense to ignore him.
But, our rooster Buster, who has ruled the henhouse
Before I was born, watches the younger rooster.
Buster is so black that he turns blue
When the sun strikes his feathers;
Spending more time patrolling his yard
Than preening a novel of feathers.
He loves fighting more than he loves living.
While Ted loves preening more than he loves
Power-driving another rooster's head into the dust.

Ted's head slowly swells in its brainpan
Of golden thoughts & grand expectations of himself;
He's tired of serving as Buster's wingman.
This morning he spreads his wings
& loves the power of his own wingspan.
He hatches a plan on the spot, a bird-brained
Idea that one contemplates when it's time

To serve as anchorman of his own life.
He approaches Buster, who watches a line
Of newly hatched chicks who are living
Testimonials that he is the lead man
In his henhouse narrative.

Buster, who loves fighting more than he loves living,
Does not expect a feather-flying brawl so early in the morning.
He has just summoned the sun from its bed with his signature
Growl, a southern drawl signaling all of us to shake a tail feather
& begin our day with focus and grit.
Signaling to his wingman Ted to begin foraging.
But Ted covers so much ground in so little time
That Buster, wild-eyed & tongue-tied,
Stalls before he could start his own motor.
As if his mind is lost in a maze of previous brawls,
When he had been a hot knife slicing through butter.
When he was young, limber & sweet to the bone.
Buster loses his footing & loses focus.
Ted's sharp spurs free Buster of his feet
& one wing. Without flight.

With neither feet nor footing,

Buster growls a deathbed plea…

Watches his blue-black chicks with one wild eye

As Ted Of The Sky falls on his sweet back.

## *First Day*

Teacher buzzes around our classroom
Cracking windows ("It smells like a zoo In here").
We sit stone-still in her warm tomb.

She pumps her atomizer. (What kind of voodoo
Is she spraying over our heads, I wonder?)
She sprays, sprays. Covers us in a sweet pest-proof

Film. I cough. Mom had sprayed our atomizer
To kill dirt daubers/foolish flies/mosquitoes -
All which died on the spot. Teacher is a whirling

Blue blur, spraying row by row by row by row.
If this kills flies, what about my next thought?
Salt sprinkled in her shoes will break her mojo.

## *Butter Knife*

*For Dianne*

Each morning my dad stands in front of the mirror, above our bathroom sink; his coffee cup brims with hot soapy suds, bubbles & a light lemon scent. He picks up his brown badger brush, lathers & mops his freckled face, which disappears under the gravity of soapy suds & lemon. Who is this man whose face is now covered in steaming snow, standing in my dad's floppy slippers? I offer my face only to him; he mops my face with the soapy brush & I too become someone other than his son – ten toes splayed, cooling & proofing on cool blue linoleum. Lemony suds make dad & me twins in this only room in the world this time of the morning. He picks up a straight razor & shaves away his snow-white bubbling beard. I pick up my butter knife & lift it to my face. But I wait/hesitate before I shave the hot snow off my face. I like that we are twins in this only room in the world. If only for a few seconds every morning.

## *Mr. Tin Ears*
*For Franklin*

I walk, shoulders-squared,

To the front of the classroom.

I'm in the first grade

& my teacher smells like cheese.

She taps the blackboard

With a yellow yardstick, her best friend.


Earlier, she had tapped my knuckles;

Said I had not been listening to her.

How would she know

Whether or not I'd listened to her -

Unless she borrowed my ears?

I had not loaned my ears to anyone.

Dad had taught me not to loan

What I could not live without or afford to

Purchase a second time on my own dime.

"Mr. Tin Ears, what letter is this?"

She asks me, tapping the blackboard with her yard stick.

As if she's tapping a snare drum.

The "J" curves like Charlie Parker's saxophone.

"That's no letter –

This is an alto saxophone – this is Bird's ax!!"

I respond. She turns beet red,

Draws her thin lips into a single line.

Her yardstick stops drumming.

Immediately, I stick my hands into both pockets.

## Lead Belly

After church, I hustle home & remove my mason jar from underneath our front porch. Last night, I had filled the quart-sized jar with fireflies. Inside the jar, the walls are sticky with peach rendering from last fall's preserves. Last night, I had been a midnight miner with fireflies flying around my head. I sported my dad's baseball cap, so that I could think like he thinks. I stalked through darkness - through honeysuckles, grape vines, thistles & thorns. When a firefly had lighted on a leaf, a bush, a basket or a ball, I placed the glass mouth of the jar over it & scooped it into the jar with the brass lid. After two hours, countless fireflies glowed within the jar and transformed the jar into a lantern of living light. I held the lantern to the night air, delighted that their light passed through the sugared walls of the jar. I hankered to be weighted by as much light as Lead Belly belly's had been filled with lead, longing, buck shot, BBs, etc., etc., etc. So, I pressed the jar to my stomach & I rose to the tips of my toes as slowly/as easily/as biscuits rising in an oven. I hoped their bellies would pulse syncopated light through the glass walls into my stomach, until my stomach glowed. But now the fireflies are dead, rattling around my jar like BBs. I untwist the brass lid, sniff inside the jar & inhale a dead sweetness. I am hungry. I drop the jar & round the house towards the kitchen at top speed; in my rearview mirror, I spot Jesse Owens & Wilma Rudolph trailing/eating my dust. Rounding the corner of the house, I glimpse the chopping block which holds our back yard in place; sunlight catches the blade of my mother's perfect axe; draws my eyes to the white chicken resting on the chopping block - hypnotized by its own fear, offering its own neck. Simple as a bag of sugar. In the arc of my mother's perfect swing, she pulls sunlight & our hunger to the edge of her perfect blade & lops off the chicken's head, which tumbles off the block like a wood chip. She pitches the chicken to the grass and it bobs about the yard, bleeding out, looking for its own head. Red blood washes white feathers & teaches me no one/nothing lives forever.

## *Hope*
*For Pandora*

Each bed is the best bed

In our shotgun-house.

Floating on roaming blues

& raw rippling regret.

A Word nudges me, without

Apology. Without articulating

Its expectations. Then, it elbows

Me in the ribs. It has no face, no home.

No last name. Its head had never

Rested on a pillow its traveling life.

Has no need for food - handles

Neither fork nor spoon but lives,

Thrives on an internal eternal light.

Which bears its own fruit & hooch.

The soles of its shoes are as thin

As my winding sheet - but its shoes

Will never wear out. Walked

Thinner but never walked-out.

## *Camel Knees*

You have to kneel beside your bed to pray.
Unless you kneel, God won't hear your prayer.
That's the rule-I don't care how old you are
Or the number of items on your prayer list.

Our wood floor is rock-hard & it hurts my knees.
Sends needles up my legs. My knees are red hot.
Once I touched dad's knees & his knees were
As hard as my pet rock, whose name is Rock.

Then, I touched my knees. My knees weren't
Half as hard as dad's; marshmallows are firmer.
But my knees are brown like his - not milk white.
Where can I get a set of camel knees like dad's?

## *Prayer Chain*

Who should I pray for tonight?

Who should I skip tonight?

God must have two very very big big ears

Because everybody prays to him, year

After year after year. All at the same time.

His ears are bigger than the elephant

Ears growing in my mom's flower bed.

It takes at least a trillion junebugs

To cover one of her elephant ears.

A June bug could fly this prayer

To God (who listens to even stones)

& make heaven his honey home.

## *Lunch*

Teacher divides our class in half with her yellow yardstick. Like God had separated the waters of the Red Sea with His giant thumb for the Hebrew children: Students with tin lunch boxes line up along the right wall; the sun had burned their faces raspberry red more than once, so she watched them with a mother's eye. Maybe if she had kissed their cheeks before recess, the sun would not have been so mean to them. I didn't burn in the sun. I wash my face in the sun & my skin remains red like my grandfather's. My grandmother's skin is darker than the coffee she drinks, straight, no cream, no sugar.

I am numbered with my classmates lining the left wall, without tin lunch boxes. Without roaming mother-eye. My teacher distributes us paper *lunch cards* which cover the cost of a meal & a carton of white milk. "Poor students lead off to the lunchroom today," she sings, pointing the yellow yardstick at me & mine. Poor? I had never heard this word. It was a heavy word because it lays on her tongue heavy, the way a tablespoon of honey weighs down my tongue to the bottom of my mouth. We had not sounded out that word (p-o-o-r) on the blackboard, which could hold more words than I could fit into my pockets.

When I arrive home, my mom is walking room to room. After she cleans a room the room always seems bigger. She swept away cobwebs from the corners of the ceiling & the corners moved closer to heaven - where the man with the Giant Thumb lives. I wonder if his thumb could part my teacher's hair down the center of her head like he had parted the Red Sea, because she wears the same hair style every day: pulled back in a bun so tight her eyes bulge from their soft sockets. Does Giant Thumb keep a clean house? If He needs help & if she could make it back before church this evening, my mom could make the corners of his house recede, beyond rain & rainbows. Mom could make better use of His sky. Make room for more than one sun during the day & room for more than one moon at night. Softer nights. Fatter stars. His stars were small enough to fit into my front pocket along with my crayons. (Tonight, I will ask God to name a star for my mom.)

Walking towards me, our pine-wood floors extend an inch under each of her steps: How long it will take our hallway to reach heaven? "My teacher says we're poor," I say. "Really? Really? Well, I didn't catch that story on the noon news & I've had the television going all day," she says. So, I guess it's no big deal after all that we're poor. She shakes out her new quilt. For the past two weeks, I'd seen her & several church sisters hunched over pieces of flour sacks, old shirts and pants. Humming through mouthfuls of stick pins. Had they learned to hum something from nothing like God, who surely had a song stirring in his head while he pieced together the sun without burning his thumb and other fingers? Shaking out the quilt,

Mom almost shakes off the moon & the stars they'd sown on the top quilt. Mom folds the quilt & places it in the trunk at the foot of my bed. I had wondered where the big-faced moon & those skinny stars had hidden during the day.

## *Blue Plate*
For Sam Powell


My grandfather names me Blue Plate

While I am still eating from bowls.


When I'd thought white lightning poured from the sky

As the devil beat his wife with braided thunderbolts


(Now, I know white lightning percolates under the bed

Of my parents like the coffee pot on our white wood stove).


The nickname, Blue Plate, sticks with me, but

The actual plate models in my mother's hutch.


Initially, its center was a deep, royal blue

But slowly faded to robin's-egg blue, paling


With the facile passing of each morning biscuit.

A deeper smoke-blue rims this familial plate.

Across the heart of the plate there is a hair-thin crack.

He wolfs about the plate's age & its porcelain demeanor:

How the most bitter of breads will sweeten if it rests

Upon the blue plate a few seconds after the sun rises.

How it's been carried from blue house to shot house,

From white folks' tables to colored tables, as if it's

A robin's egg. But he never mentions the crack.

## *Canary*

For Henry (a/k/a Junior)

The yellow Cadillac idles in our sidewalk,

Perched like a yellow Canary on a tree limb.

Topping her off with gas is a cakewalk

For my dad who has folding money to lend;

Works triple shifts without breaking a sweat,

Shoveling a mountain of rock into an oven -

Whose cast-iron belly is bloated but bottom-less.

With each load, the blade of his shovel thins, shines;

He'll have to buy another to dig his own grave.

Unless God calls his number sometime soon.

But he has no time to think about death,

Standing flatfooted before a mountain of ore.

## *Leather Seats*

This is not Red's first yellow Cadillac

& it won't be his last. Every check

His mouth writes is good money in the bank.


Red is no joke, but the real deal – with cash to spare.

It's one of a school of cool, newly used cars

Resting on boss rims & his unshakeable faith.


Red believes a car is still in kindergarten

Until it's eaten its first 300,000 miles of ethereal

Interstate & burped bellies of gas from its tailpipe.


The Cadillac thrum thrums like a Singer Sewing

Machine, which idles for only him, coughing a gust

Of blue smoke from its cracked tailpipe, spiraling


Above the roof of our feather house. He

Is a man who handles his car, his blues

& his nine-to-five without breaking a sweat.

He backs the canary onto our broad street & pumps

The gas, just as Howlin' Wolf growls sweet blues

From Red's eight-track player. Burning blue tracks

In Red's tongue. He recently put new shoes

On his canary & knows she won't belly-out

On the umbilical roads leading to Memphis.

Its buckled leather seats are the bible for luxury;

But he initially squirms a bit in the driver's seat

Which is always grained by another man's butt.

## *Hunger Bone*

Grandfather's skin color is roasted, coffee-bean black.

His color is so rich you can taste it with one glance.

I'm as red as he is the color of roasting coffee beans.

O to be like him - his skin wrapped around my bones.

I want to be just like my grandfather

Who worked in a boneyard as a boy.

Smuggling soup bones home in brown bags.

In the marrow of his mind, life is life

& what lies in between can be hairy regret.

And a chance to make your woman smile.

Make her face shine - like it says in the Bible.

He learns to love while stirring bones in brine.

I want to be just like my grandfather.

Consider his love for words a proverb

For living my life in our shared skin,

A shared agenda beyond paternal DNA:

I would speak words first softened in his mouth,

Which is a sugarhouse for each syllable & sound.

His words have the power to part the moon

From its poorhouse blues, but I memorize them.

O Let my blood drain into a vat of cow tendons & clarity.

O Let his light words (their unbent intent)

Redeem the hoof & phalange of time so that

His life is full/complete, beyond a skeletal purpose.

He only spoke words first softened in God's mouth.

Whose every word accomplishes His purpose.

Never return to His perfectly balanced lips,

Never sour in Grandfather's stomach, even if

It cuts him until he almost bleeds out:

No man is perfect, whether you stir a vat of fat,

Fuse bone and tendon or bill clients by the minute.

Real men stand on God's word without question.

## *The Size of a Cowpea*

Grandfather's home is more than a kingdom of bone.
Its roof is not a tin clip-on
Because he hand-picked each tin sheet &
Paid with silver coins he'd earned stirring a vat

Of huffs, craniums, and hip-bones of cows.
America does not give coupons to men of color.
He knows this. He chews this. He responds
By stirring bones & cartilage in their own juices

Until the cow's shoulders, hips & ribs are jelly.
His home is more than a kingdom of bone.
He hand-picks each nail, each holy plank
To match the picture God whispered into

His ear one night while he slept in relief;
He doesn't press God for a road map -
As he has grown to recognize God's voice,
Exercising a living faith the size of a cowpea.

His home is more than a kingdom of bone.

His chest is no wider than a teenaged boy

But it's ribbed to swing John Henry's hammer.

Raising a praise-song from the sweet lips of his

Sweetheart with each swing. What else could unhinge

A lover's leather tongue & seal each board, door & window

In his shotgun house? Nothing but His plan & a few fingers

Of ten penny nails, thin doors & a simple, naked faith.

## *Blame it on the Blues*

Grandfather's right index finger misses a joint,

Gnawed to a black nub at the Piano Factory.

His supervisor, benefactor of this blood-work,

Records the pound of Grandfather's flesh as a mere fracture;

Issues a letter of unsatisfactory performance to him

& a reprimand of industrial import & magnitude summed

In a simple sentence on official company letterhead.

The supervisor, a glutton for industrial accidents,

Blames my Grandfather's love for low-down blues

As the culprit for *this* bleeding industrial drama:

"The coloreds are often distracted by the rambling

Music stirring in their craniums. Blues is their Bible."

Grandfather, right-handed since birth, could not sign

His letter of reprimand, so an X becomes his signet ring

For the tenor of his piano-making days.

Blame it on the blues, blame it on the blues.

## *Knee Babies*

A threader at the Piano Factory

(Not blues rambling in his head)

Had gnawed Grandfather's finger

To a black nub of familial sacrifice.

Whether a pound of flesh

An error of freshman judgment

A miscalculation of torque

(Even if you dismiss this thread

Of an argument), an error bleeds

Into the heartbeat of life with ease

& without excuse: Never again

Will he lift & shoulder a casket.

Since they are knee babies,

Standing at their mothers' knees

Black boys are raised to swing

Caskets from sultry morning suns

To lumbering moon-struck nights.

They'd listened to their fathers' sacred

Songs stir a widow's heart as they lifted

& swung sweet chariots into the sleeve

Of a hungry grave: a life-long call & response.

Their fathers' black patent leather shoes had navigated

The same unsatisfied graveyards as did their fathers.

These men don't sell wolf tickets, Avon, or trinkets.

They love the flavor of love & sugar-drunk faith.

Their shoulders, baked by sun & bronzed

By patience, swing caskets from one bank

Of the Mississippi River to the Nile River.

## *Brothers in Bone*

I hunger for a right index finger

Like my grandfather's:

Missing one familial joint.

Missing one clear nail.

It would be my tribal mark.

Not a token for capitalism

But a familial marker of black

Men, scored in my human flesh.

We'd be brothers in blues & bone.

Our ancestral song written in pain

Will be a holy psalm on the tongues

For those who follow, survive & thrive.

## *Upon Seeing My First Kiss*

Is he trying to return her

Words into her mouth?

Had what she mouthed been

So bitter to his taste buds?


Or, is she trying to share a secret

With him? If so, she should be speaking

Into his ear (not his mouth)

So she won't have to repeat herself.

## *Falcon*

Grandfather's Red Falcon chugs & tugs us along back roads, which had been cut first for wagons. He riffles down a two-way road as if it's one-way all the way. His one good tire has less tread than my red high-top Converse; the other three tires are maypops – bald as apples & may pop at any time. The falcon coughs white smoke from its cracked tailpipe. Levels off at 45 m.p.h. - a smooth ride. Only cruising a Cadillac would guarantee a smoother groove. He has more than Falcon money in his pockets. His railroad retirement check may not stretch four weeks, but he's learned he can't change the number of days in a month: no matter how hard he presses God. He may not have Cadillac money, but I know he got deep pockets. I know. I know. I'd hidden my red diesel truck in his pocket. My yellow yo-yo that I could make *walk the dog* even if the dog didn't wanna walk. My crayons. Marbles. Jawbreakers which don't break nothing. I'd hidden a herd of buffalo-head nickels & big-head silver dollars in his back pocket. (I know he hides dimes in the brims of his hats. If I wear his hat will I think the same thoughts that he thinks?).

My pockets are small, almost too small for my eraser. An egg won't fit without its shell exploding into a scramble of yolk & frustration. But my pocket is big enough to hold my name, without one letter sticking out. I whisper my name into my pocket because Mom says I have to remember my name in case I get lost. Grandfather's name is too big for my pocket:

Grandfather Willie Sam Powell from Coldwater, Mississippi. Where the water is sweeter than honey, but not the white folks.

If I had a *real* hat (not this red baseball cap), I'd keep his name in my brim. The closer his name is to my head the more I can think about him, think what he's thinking while he's thinking it. Take this next curve, for instance. Will his falcon make it - without rustling one red feather? Or will she belly-out? He presses the gas pedal with his iron foot.

## *Haiku*

"If you find my name
On your way home. Please, keep it,
Until you return."

## *Brogans*

My smile is too big for my face. My hands are too small. I need two hands to carry one egg. Grandfather had carried blues so long in his head that worry lines had creased his forehead & cracked every plate in his kitchen. His every day walk draws music from mockingbirds that lean into his day to check out his swagger.

I want to look like my Grandfather. More so than I want to look like myself. I look into my mourning mirror: Close my eyes early. Count to twenty twice! By ones & then by twos. **Will** that my red skin darkens a deep, roasting coffee bean like his. Then, when he'd sip his morning cup he'd think of me - minus cream/sugar/ & other thinners. I will settle for a skin of wet tea leaves even, swirling in the bottom of his evening cup. My lids pop open - one at a time. I am almost paralyzed by the possibility that I'd see only myself again. (Before this mourning mirror I'd learned the draw & failure of hope). It's me again. No second skin this morning. No miracle rebirth like Nicodemus who'd shaken like a leaf on a tree when Christ opened his eyes with the truth & washed Nicodemus' face, feet & heart - white as snow. If Nicodemus had asked Grandfather how a grown man could be born a second time, he would've told brother Nicodemus every time you read God's Word, if your heart is right & no caul covers your eyes.

Each morning, I shuffle around his shotgun-house, room to room, navigating his oversized black brogans. His brogans would swallow my feet whole like that whale had swallowed Jonah - whole. Unlike Jonah, I will not let my blues seal my lips shut or turn my back to God, who made my back. Maybe not this morning, but soon these rooms will shrink a shoe size or so if I keep walking with my head up. Walk the way a man walks when he knows what he has is all he really truly needs: who can walk with two concrete blocks for shoes from Memphis to Chicago to buy a stick of rag bologna & make it back on time to usher at church; who can walk from Memphis to Mississippi for a sip of water because Mississippi water is sweeter than Tennessee water & who can walk to heaven and ask Nicodemus or Jonah to borrow a can of Dapper Dan.

Until then, I will shamble along these pine boards that creak & moan with gout. I'm slow-walking this floor so much that it will memorize my name, whether I'm barefooted or sporting my dad's steel-toed shoes. Walking them down like a grown man walks down a mountain to dust before his morning meal.

I wonder at what age Grandfather had fit, filled & perfected these black brogans on my feet? Wonder when I will? Until then, I'll be stomping blues from every board.

## *Underwriter (risk, insurance, blues, etc., etc.)*

I snake under our kitchen table on my back,

A salty cracker (*show bread*) between my teeth;

The salt on the cracker preserves

My every move & reserves the universe

Of my canvas – a dimpled wooden surface

Underneath my mom's mahogany table.

With each chalky letter that I scribble

The mahogany table extends an inch

In white powder. With each number I score

Under my mahogany chalkboard, I take one step

Beyond fatherly lessons salved onto my tongue

By my dad and the host of bluesmen rotating

On the record player in our living room.

I'd borrowed the white chalk from my

Teacher. Each chalky letter I scribble
Is* a testament to her biblical lessons,

Spelled & parsed to fit my head. Replacing
Words salved onto my tongue. Supplanting

Blue lessons percolating in a silver coffee pot
On our white woodstove & in the bloodshot

Eyes of every underpaid black man in my town;
The harder they work the less money they earn.

I write under the table, under the six chairs standing
Erect around our kitchen table like dutiful students.

Who learn that the closer they listen to the teachings
Of this country, the less they will ever know.

Who learn they will never be invited to our nation's *table*
*Of brotherhood* as it is eternally one chair short for our kind.

I consider expanding my underwriting skills

To skywriting underneath the pews at my church

But my mom learns about my elementary enterprise

& threatens to employ a switch (her best friend) to write

Her name in cursive on my butt if I franchised

My underwriting expertise & skill to God's house.

## Fastback

Red is the fastest man on four wheels:
268 mustangs snort under his hood.
He never rests on her metallic skills.

His '68 Mustang is his life-long metal meal
& writes the schoolbook for racing, for good times.
Red, the fastest man on four rubber wheels.

Percolating on our sidewalk, the '68 seals the lips
Of any haters because Red is primed & limber
Because he never rested on her horse-powered skills.

He does not sell wolf tickets or nickel-and-dime
His friends to death. Cause it's Howlin' Wolf's job
To wolf that Red is the fastest Mustang on four wheels.

So, don't watch your watch! Don't take it so hard!
Just listen to the thunder growling under the hood
Because Red never sleeps on Fastback skills.

Flagman drops his white shirt; tires peel for show.

Red floors her & she fish-tails; punches her again & she eats

Asphalt for her morning snack. Those who'd misunderstood

Learn that Red is the fastest living man on four wheels.

A man who never rests on his Fastback skills.

## *Final Blue Note*

Lead Belly's bullet-train leaves the Memphis station with a one-way ticket to heaven, like a bat out of hell. He does not have one crumb, not one soda cracker in his pockets. He is a prodigal rooster heading home to roost with a club-foot & a trumpet corked in his throat (We will pray for him at church on Sunday).

I didn't see him, but every wagging tongue at his funeral had said that Lead Belly was as thin as a wafer & lead lined his belly by the gallons. That his reliable six string reclined alongside him in his blue casket. That the eulogy of his days could not be read in public or preached by any self-respecting preacher, especially in the presence of women and children; so, everyone just hummed hymns through a honeycomb of lies & blues.

Then, his single-shot train arrives in heaven. Lead Belly opens his eyes & jumps off the train. His reliable six string slung across shoulders and club-foot in tow. He faces twelve pearly gates, uncorks the silver trumpet in his throat & crows like my Rooster Ted, "If the fellows from the pool hall could see me now." He smiles. Lead Belly rummages through his pockets for a key to open at any one of those twelve pearly gates, but remembers he'd left every key to his name on his nightstand, next to his can of pomade. He decides to sing his way into heaven. He cradles his reliable six-string and then notices that someone had strung his guitar with six used shoelaces from his father's black brogans. Then, Lead Belly really squalls and crows, crows and squalls, squalls and crows, until a blue bird crests the sky, circles & rolls. Lead Belly then squalls his final blues: "I'm gone hitch a ride, Sweet Baby. Wake where the sun never sets. I'm gonna hitch a ride, Sweet Baby, and open my eyes where the sun don't set. Dip down low, Sweet Honey. Meet a man with no regrets. Dip down low, way down low, Sweet Honey, and sing with a real man with no regrets. Not one single regret." The blue bird circles the sun seven times, dips down, way down low & Lead Belly mounts her back. Her breast is tissue-soft. Her voice is clear as spring water. Her back is strong. Like Harriet Tubman, she's never lost a passenger. But now her wing tips are scorched, having dipped too close to the sun after Lead Belly bellowed his last blue note.

## *Prophecy*
*For Reggie*

The day before Red gives up the ghost,
    He and Uncle Miles, who is the closest
he'd ever had as a brother,
    cruises Memphis in Red's yellow Cadillac.
Uncle Miles remembers the day
    Two years later. Miles thinks,
Would bet his last lame dime
    That Red had looked from his Mercy

Seat & spotted the Reaper
    Packing Red's clothes in one brown paper
Bag. Miles wonders if the Reaper
    Had truly considered Red's life-long billing:
Fifty-nine years of parties,
    Dancing back-to-back in gambling
Joints, shake joints, smoke-filled
    Joints. Fish-fries in the county.

Dancing until sweat glistens

On his forehead, dripping down his back.
Red, shoe-less, sockless,
    an ankle bracelet of stardust.
The Reaper would have to pack
    Red's fast-foot shuffle the girls loved so
("he will make pretty babies")
    Out of hearing distance,

Out of seeing distance of parents.
    He'd snake around the prettiest;
Amazed & stumped that tiny bumps
    On their chest's fleshed to mangos.
Can the Reaper stack & pack
    Red's vinyl 45s in a brown paper bag?
And his bulky 8-track tapes
    He'd refused to throw away
Because cassettes tapes were
    Simply a fading fad; so he'd maintained his tracks
In a lavender-scented, yellow suitcase
    Under his marriage bed? No. His 45s which had revolved
On our turntable like Sunday saucers,
    Will finally replace Saturn's silent rings.

## *The Last Supper*

Plain as day, Uncle Miles says Red
    Had caught the Reaper packing his rags, records,
8-track tapes & salty regret
    Into a million brown paper bags.
Plain as day. While Uncle Miles knew
    The Reaper could pack paper bags but
Catching Red was another
    Profession requiring proper schooling:
"Red could outrun
    Any living running thing," he says,
Cradling a bottle of Wild Irish
    Rose in his lap. Though gout had crimped
Red's wrists & crippled his ankles;
    (Locked his knees on the spot)
Red would leave an atom,
    Splitting through light muslin,
Eating his exhaust & dirt.

Uncle Miles holds that day in his lap
    As if it's a child who has lost its way home;
Along with a frosted bottle
    Of sweet red wine.

He unscrews the top off the liquid
    Gold, tilts his head back into that final day
& the wine flows as a red ribbon
    Down Miles' leather throat.
Miles now wonders when the Reaper
    Will pack his paper bag? Wonders how his angel's
Wing will feel, grazing his right cheek,
    Redeeming his redeemable parts
& letting everything else
    Fall away into locked closets with no keys.
He's unsure what he most needs:
    A $2 bottle of cold wine
Pickling his liver.
    Or Red's warning – "Man we gotta get right
With the Man upstairs. Only He got
    The keys to His pearly gates.
The keys in our pockets
    Fit only our houses, our cars, trucks, work lockers.
Our keys won't fit one church
    Door - down here. Won't fit one lock
On any of His twelve gates - up there."

Plain as day, Miles remembers
    Their final supper; Red's yellow Cadillac parked
On the baseball field, its nose pointing
    Toward the left outfield - where Red had snatched
Baseballs & stars from the sky;
    His swollen ankles, retiring in his untied shoes;
The chunk of hog-head cheese
    They shared is missing five bites;
Both eye a final soda cracker;
    Howlin' Wolf squalls from 8 tracks,
Burning 4-bar blues on their tongues;
    Red's red beard is fire-red;
Hotter than an Irish Rose
    Burning a hole in Mile's stomach;
Burning hotter than Moses' burning bush
    Drawing him into a thicket of peace & worship.

# Sweet Honey in the Rock

Fourth quarter. Ten quick ticks 'til the time clock ticks down. We're down one point. Our ball. We'd rather round-ball than eat. Time to homeschool these boys. My lungs expand to a full moon. These simple boys set a half-court press. As if we're not lightning with feet! Hoping we'd cough up the ball. Rock bullets the ball to Slim. Rock is short for Peter as in rocky road/as in rolling rockin' robin/as in rolling stone/as in On This Rock I Will Build My Church. Slim, who is weak as water with the girls but all man round-balling, riffles the ball to Rock. Rock can ball with the best of them. Our dollar-store sneakers navigate buckled, hardwoods with the skills of a master. This court is our center. Center of our universe/where creation creates/why Romare Bearden had dipped his brush & withdrawn fire-hot blues. Rock fakes a pass to me, the mid-court man, but rockets the leather bullet to JoeJoe, who bullets it cross court to Dozier, deflating their half-hearted, half-court press. Seven ticks on the clock. Rock is cool/icebox cool/ refrigerator cool/ freezer cool. No one can beat Rock when he's in his zone. Not even Yo-Yo Ma, priming the cello between his legs until her four strings surrender Hannibal from history's iron footnote. They set a weak 2-1-2 zone like we don't know *this* game/like we can't read a pre-school zone/like we don't round-ball in my backyard until Hannibal's 37 elephants trumpet our names across the Pyrenees/across the Rhone's troubled waters/across the Alps/crowning my backboard, in my back yard. Where our three-pointers had dropped like rain before they were called three-pointers. When we ball we change our minds at the same time. If Rock smiles we know it's time to take care of bizzness. Time to school & retool these boys like they're first graders. Dozier rockets the ball to Rock, knowing this moment has had Rock's name on it before dirt was dirt. At the key, Rock rocks on the balls of his feet. He was born for this second, this master scene. Just like black men born & bred to swing caskets from creation into the open mouths of hungry graves. Rock pulls up for a jump shot. He releases the ball off the tips of his pea-picking fingers & his release is sweet. Sweet like my girl is sweet/sweet honey in the rock sweet/sugar-water sweet.

## *Grace*
For Robert

I am a sophomore at Morehouse & just learned my tin ears are different sizes: a paternal fact my dad had dropped into my lap earlier this morning, following a final drag on a *Kool*. But now, we stand on the lip of a bridge arching the Tallahatchie River. He can see for miles with naked eyes; as Moses had seen from one bank of the Red Sea to a land flowing with milk & honey – without contact lenses, without eyeglasses, with simple faith. I barely see a few feet beyond the steel lip of this bridge wearing both contacts & glasses – at the same time. Dad pulls out a .45 & points to a red bucket in the distance; the ilk of bucket Albert King had used to lug left-handed, cotton-picking blues from dusty Mississippi cotton fields / through red-hot juke joints in Memphis/ into empty kitchens in Chicago - without spilling one blue blessed drop. Target practice time! My minor confession: This is not my strong suit. As a matter of fact, I don't own a suit. I decline, respectfully. Though I have only a dollar in my pocket, I still have my pride. He sweetens the deal: once he shoots, he'll join my team & the two of us will try to best him at his finest game. I ask for a list of his references: I can't have just anyone joining my team. I may have only four quarters in my front pocket, but I still have my pride. I may be nearsighted, simultaneously wearing contact lenses & eyeglasses; my right ear may be larger than my left – but I still have to consider my options. Not to mention my portfolio of suppositions, equations & brave sincere bull-headed defiance. Dad aims at the red bucket, pulls the trigger - as if beckoning the bucket closer to him. A bullet rips air & strikes its red target. After I explain the job pays little but carries plenty of overtime, we settle on the familial terms of our verbal contract. Dad discloses his weaknesses & cheats himself - without hesitation. I'm as tight-lipped as a pocket watch: I know what time it is. An hour later, copper shell casings outline where we stand on the bridge; each empty casing is an eyewitness of grit & grace arching a living river.

# Epilogue

## *Morning Psalm*

For Omega Psi Phi Fraternity, Incorporated

Father God, Heavenly Father
Standing before your throne
Kneeling before your throne of Grace
Are your earthly sons filled with heavenly aspiration.

We lift this day to you because it is your creation.
We lift our lives to you because you created us.
Anoint this day with your holy power.
Anoint us for your purpose this very hour.

Teach us! And we will love wholeheartedly.
Teach us to love fully & completely.
May your Holy word guide every day.
May your grace cover each & every way.

## *About the Author*

Gregory Powell graduated from Morehouse College in 1987 with a degree in journalism and worked several years as a news reporter at the *Memphis Business Journal, Jackson Sun* and the *Commercial Appeal*; he earned a Doctor of Laws Degree from the University of Wisconsin-Madison Law School in 1994; a Masters of Fine Arts Degree in Creative Writing from the University of Alabama-Tuscaloosa in 2004, and a Masters of Divinity from the School of Divinity at Regent University in 2014.

He has worked as a labor and employment law attorney for the federal government almost twenty years. He currently works as Professor of Ethics and Leadership Development at William Seymour College, and operates his own labor and employment law consulting firm. Previously, his poetry has been published in *Callaloo, African American Review, Langston Hughes Review, Arkansas Review, story south (on-line journal), Antietam Review, Poem, touchstone, Mosaic, Lake Effect* and *Tar Wolf Review*.

He is currently writing a cycle of seven plays that address Civil Rights, Voting Rights, Employee Rights, Working Conditions, Race Relations, and Religion in the 20th Century. The Aldridge Repertory Theatre, Inc., presented a Staged Reading of his first play, "*Ruby's Harmonicas & Pianos, Incorporated,*" at Downtown Theatre in Birmingham, Alabama. This work Bloody Sunday in Selma, Alabama, unions and employee rights; the second play in the cycle, *"Turpentine Beans Bones Blues,"* set in rural Georgia in 1928, examines Convict Leasing. *"No Honey in the Rock,"* is set in Memphis and explores institutional racism, unions, and employee rights, against the backdrop of the Memphis Sanitation Strike.

Gregory is currently researching and writing the fourth play, *"Fire in my Bones,"* which examines the genesis of the Student Nonviolent Coordinating Committee. A fifth play in the cycle, *Levi Processing & Packaging, Inc.*, is still in the formative stage.

Gregory can be contacted at gpowell65@gmail.com to facilitate creative writing workshops, lectures, and staged readings.

www.ingramcontent.com/pod-product-compliance
Lightning Source LLC
LaVergne TN
LVHW020937090426
835512LV00020B/3405